THE POWER OF

DEVELOPING GROWTH MINDSET
THROUGH POSITIVE SELF-TALK

DeVante Wynn, MBA, MAT.

A SPECIAL THANKS TO...

My family and friends...

who have supported me and pushed me out of my comfort zone. I always said that I wanted to write a book, and you all encouraged and inspired me to do so.

A SPECIAL THANKS TO...

My Creator...

I thank God for the vision he gave me and for blessing me with the perseverance to see it through. I hope that He has spoken through me to one of you readers. In Your name, we pray... Amen.

A SPECIAL
THANKS TO...

YOU.

Yes, YOU! I thank you for taking the time to purchase and read this book. I have poured my heart into these pages and hope that at least one thing on at least one page inspires you to chase your wildest dreams. You have the power of achieving anything you dream of, but you just haven't figured out how... YET!

DeVante Wynn, MBA, MAT.

A NOTE TO THE READER ...

This is not a book for people interested in getting rich quick. It is, however, an opportunity for you to be introduced to concepts vital to the success of developing a growth mindset. If you are someone who has significant concerns regarding the treatment of a mental health condition, please seek medical or professional guidance.

FOREWORD

So I bet you're wondering, why the astronaut? Why would someone writing and speaking on the *Power of Yet* use an astronaut as a visual point of reference? The word astronaut derives from the Ancient Greek word *astron* which means "star." We all know that stars appear to shine the brightest in the midst of some of the darkest skies. According to Oxford, an astronaut is a person <u>trained, equipped, and deployed</u> by a human spaceflight program to serve as a member aboard a spacecraft. An astronaut explores the unknown and pushes the limits of our universe to discover the most beautiful and intricate specimens of our galaxy. An astronaut defies most human physics, even the odds of gravity, to establish new boundaries for all humankind.

Now, you may not be a literal astronaut but you have been trained, equipped, and deployed into this world with amazing gifts and talents. You have the ability to explore the unknown and push the limits of your personal universe to discover the most beautiful and intricate parts of yourself. You will be the person in your family to defy the odds and establish new boundaries. You will be the one to restore hope where it has been lost. You have the ability to be somebody's shining light in their darkest moment.

You can accomplish your wildest dreams and inspire countless people in the process. You can and you will, but you haven't figured out how... YET! The Power of Yet is rooted in your attentiveness to the details of your life. It is in the details that we retrieve the keys to our greatest successes. Speaking of details, take one more look at the front cover...

The astronaut invests his attention in the details of his reflection. That is the purpose and goal of this book. Can you capture, in the details of your reflection, the daily habits, ineffective self-talk, and incompatible environments that have contributed to your current stagnation? Can you hold yourself accountable to make the necessary changes as outlined in this book?

I challenge you to be real with yourself and make the necessary adjustments to your habits that will put you closer to where you want to be. Maybe you haven't considered how your habits, self-talk, and environment affect you. For many, you know how these factors contribute to your current position but you just haven't figured out how to adjust them for positive outcomes...YET!

Finally, pay attention to the background. Look at all the blank space. Look at all the open canvas. Did you notice all that room? Can you see all the opportunity in this space? I hope so. I want you to feel safe in the mental space that this book will put you in and safe in the fact that you know that the author is walking this journey with you. None of us have this thing called "Life" figured out, but each day we wake up is a new opportunity. An opportunity to create, to explore, to inquire, and to discover. A new opportunity to share your gift with the world.

Maybe you don't know what your gift is or maybe you do know but are too afraid to share it. Regardless of your reason, I challenge you to step outside of your comfort zone and to use this space as your canvas. Use this space boldly and uniquely, even if you don't know how to use it... YET! When you commit to this book and put the strategies in place, you **will** see a difference in your mindset. You **will** learn how to manage your habits, self-talk, and environment! You **will** develop a growth mindset! You **will** accomplish your wildest dreams! You **will** do all of those great things and so much more, but you haven't done them... YET!

INTRODUCTION

PART I
INTRODUCTION

"Mindset is a set of beliefs that
shape how you make sense of the
world and yourself."

What determines your thought
pattern? How often do you have
negative thoughts? Do you notice how
they affect you? Kendra Cherry, an
author and educational consultant
focused on helping students learn
about psychology, defines mindset as
a "set of beliefs that shape how you
make sense of the world and yourself."
She continues to say that the mindset

"influences how you think, feel, and behave in any given situation." If your mindset is what determines your outlook on life, how important is it to understand what your mindset can and should do for you?

According to a 2017 study by the National Science Foundation, approximately 80% of our thoughts are considered "negative." EIGHTY PERCENT! That means four out of every five impulses that pass through our brain carry a negative effect or connotation. That same study claims that most humans have between 12,000 and 50,000 thoughts per day. I'm no math whiz, but I know that is way too many negative thoughts floating around. We must be intentional when redirecting our energy and our focus.

When discussing the intentionality of redirecting those thoughts and how to handle them, Carol Dweck is the Zen master. Carol Dweck is an American psychologist who teaches courses in motivation, personality, and social development. In her 2006 book titled *Mindset: The New Psychology of Success*, she first introduced the concept of "growth mindset." According to Dweck, people can have either fixed or growth mindsets. Those with fixed mindsets believe that their basic qualities are fixed traits. She describes those with growth mindsets as "people who believe their most basic abilities can be developed through dedication and hard work." One of the best indicators to identify which mindset you have is your self-talk.

Self-talk is talk or thoughts directed at oneself. According to Merriam-Webster, "Studies show that both negative and positive self-talk influence performance." Self-talk can create distance between our physical and mental beings. Think about the last time you were struggling to complete a task and had to call yourself back to attention. "Come on, DeVante! You can do this...." Often that phrase helps me refocus and relieves any anxiety that may have built up as my struggles continued.

Notice how I called myself by name. When speaking in third person, it creates distance between the physical "I" and the mental "you." Speaking in third person during self-talk often gives us a bird's eye view perspective of our own lives. In his 2018 book titled *The Science of Self Talk,* Ian Tuhovsky describes why it is so important to identify that "critical inner voice." He explains how self-talk isn't random. Tuhovsky details that our self-talk is a reflection of our thoughts and emotions, and this self-talk exhibits patterns that repeat. There can be positive and negative self-talk;

both of which have their own unique effects on the human mind and body.

In previous years, somebody who practiced negative self-talk was referred to as a "perfectionist," but modern psychology coaches have moved away from the term as it glorifies speaking negatively to yourself. We often are our own biggest critic and the way we feel and speak about who we are and what we want to accomplish has a direct effect on how we continue to pursue whatever passion is being explored at the time.

Those who were known for their uberpositive outlook on life were often referred to as phony or artificial. Most people agree that nobody is capable of being that positive all the time. What most people don't realize is that those who seem to be "Positive Pat" work very hard to maintain that thought process and outlook. Positive Pat has figured out a way to be intentional in controlling his thoughts and altering his speech. There is no magic trick that Pat is pulling off every day and there is no secret potion to be drunk. Positive Pat has simply discovered the **power of yet**. You are going to figure it out, you will achieve great things, you are going to be more successful than your wildest dreams. You just haven't figured out how... YET!!

GROWTH
vs
FIXED
MINDSETS

PART II
GROWTH vs FIXED MINDSETS

"A person with a growth mindset believes that their most basic traits and abilities can be developed through hard work and dedication."

"People can be aware or unaware of their mindsets, but they can have a profound effect on learning achievement, skill acquisition, personal relationships, professional success, and many other dimensions of life."

Written by Carol Dweck, this quote speaks to her work that defines mindset as a self-perception or self-theory that people hold about themselves. Dweck first introduced the concept of growth mindset back in 2006 when she published *Mindset: The New Psychology of Success*. In this book, Dweck explained the difference between growth and fixed mindsets and then shared different characteristics for both.

People with fixed mindsets believe that their most basic traits and abilities are fixed traits that cannot be developed. There's one word that comes to mind when I think of the characteristics of someone with a fixed mindset: **Settle**.

People with fixed mindsets usually settle with how life is going and think they must settle for the cards they have been dealt. They believe that anything that happens to them is never their fault and they can't do anything to control the situation. They also believe that the universe is conspiring against them in ways that they cannot dispute.

In simpler terms, a person with a fixed mindset might be described as pessimistic. The pessimism in a person with a fixed is that they struggle with the basic tasks of each day. They also find it challenging to give effort because they have already accepted their predetermined outcome of the situation as finite and unresponsive to change. The character of a person with a fixed mindset is almost always revealed in how they handle criticism or respond to adversity. Ultimately, a person with a fixed mindset struggles to combat the large number of negative thoughts we have on a daily basis. The opposite is the case for people with growth mindsets.

People with growth mindsets believe that their most basic traits and abilities can be developed through hard work and dedication. They believe that where they are and what they have is just the <u>starting point</u>. One word that comes to mind when I think of the characteristics of someone with a growth mindset: **Progress**. They believe that the universe is working in their favor. Those with a growth mindset believe that they are the captain of their fate and the master of their soul. Those with a growth mindset believe that skills and talent can be built through hard work and dedication, so they strive to learn something new or be one percent better each day.

In simpler terms, a person with a growth mindset might be described as optimistic. The optimism in the person with a growth mindset embraces challenges and is hoping to learn from mistakes. In order to improve their daily performance and limit their shortcomings, people with growth mindsets seek and appreciate feedback in most cases. The optimism in a person with a growth mindset strives to see the opportunity in every obstacle and the chance in the midst of every challenge. The optimist doesn't receive failure as a definite end, but responds to it with an understanding that the task at hand is just something that they haven't figured out... YET!

Those with a growth mindset will have more positive self-talk than the pessimistic person with a fixed mindset. When adversity strikes, those with a growth mindset speak life into the situation and focuses on solutions.

Those optimistic people with growth mindsets search for the silver lining, in hopes of finding the positive aspect in difficult spaces. The pessimistic people with fixed mindsets struggle to overcome tough times because their focus, energy, and self-talk is all negative. When problems arise, people with fixed mindsets rarely put any effort into finding solutions and often focus on how dreary things seem. To achieve the success you desire, you must be optimistic, you must speak life into tough situations, and you must develop a growth mindset.

Before we go any further, let me be clear. I do not want to suggest that you overlook the real of what you are seeing and/or experiencing, but I encourage you not to become engulfed in the feelings that might encourage extreme, overwhelming pessimism.

REAL TALK
ABOUT
SELF-TALK

PART III
REAL TALK ABOUT SELF-TALK

"You're going to figure everything out. You just ain't figured out how YET! Don't worry though because you will."

How many times have you made a mistake? How often do you respond in a negative manner? I may not know you personally, but I am willing to bet that your usual response is to refer to yourself by some name or adjective that was not given to you at birth.

Even when joking or using the language "casually" this habit can be detrimental. The problem with that sort of talk is that your brain can't tell the difference. When you receive information, whether internally or externally, your brain processes it the same way. Studies have proven that self-regulation or "self-talk" usually happens from one of two perspectives, but both have similar effects on the mental and emotional state.

We often use the first-person perspective of "I'm so stupid," or "The universe hates me!" However, some people speak to themselves in third person where they use their preferred pronoun or own name(s). I know I am notorious for screaming, "Come on, Wynn!" when frustrated or needing some motivation. Regardless of the perspective from which you speak, the results can be very impactful. The biggest difference between first and third person is that speaking in third person creates distance between your actual being and your thoughts. Third person gives you a "fly-on-the-wall" perspective when speaking of yourself or to yourself. Your self-talk is inevitable and happens in cycles, but the key is in your management of that self-regulation and the acknowledgement of how it affects you.

The self-regulation cycle you're experiencing is not random. It is, rather, a constant reflection of your thoughts and emotions. I like to call this cycle the "P3 Series." The three P's that have a direct effect on our self-talk are Purpose, Power, and Performance. The P3 Series establishes how we see our abilities and appearance. The P3 Series also causes us to behave in a manner that reflects the emotions of this series.

The first P is *Purpose*. Purpose is the reason, emotion, or desire attached to an action or behavior. The purpose is why we do what we do and why we feel how we feel. The purpose is usually rooted in our self-belief, and this is where our self-talk, positive or negative, begins. When we believe that we have a reason for doing something or acting a specific way, we lean into that. When we are emotionally invested in anything, it takes a lot to remove us from it. People often spend countless hours contemplating their "purpose" for living. In the same sense, we spend a mindless amount of time deciding who we are and why we believe we are worthy of feeling that way.

The second P is *Power*. Power is the will or ability to make a difference. Notice how I didn't say "do something." I intentionally said "make a difference." It is essential that you do everything with a purpose. We all have the ability to make a significant impact on this world. We were all blessed with a unique set of skill and talent. It is up to us to explore that talent and to share it with others. When you move with the belief that every day is a learning experience and another opportunity to grow, you will start to notice your strength. Once you start to act like what you do matters, you will realize that it actually does. Once you believe that you can handle any situation thrown at you, you have discovered your power.

The final P is *Performance*.
Performance is an act or behavior that displays the psychological state of an

individual. We all display behavior that resembles how we feel about ourselves. Those who don't think they are worthy of life usually spend little to no time on grooming and hygiene. Those hoping to save money, don't usually hang out in casinos. Those who think they are destined for greatness don't do things or hang around people that jeopardize their goals and dreams. Our performance is how we display ourselves to the world.

The P3 Series happens in four steps that nobody can stop, but all of us can learn how to control. The first step in the series is the "makeup phase." In this phase, we build a picture of ourselves in our mind which shapes our self-esteem and what we believe about ourselves. We start to convince ourselves that those feelings are true and that we should behave accordingly.

The second phase is called the "performance." During the performance, we live out or portray whatever self-esteem or self-image we may carry. We dress, style, and eat like however we feel. When our self-esteem is high, we often light up rooms when we walk in. When our self-esteem is low, people can often feel the dark cloud looming over us. The performance phase is where we start to seek confirmation or denial of those personal feelings.

After the performance, we have the "feedback phase." There is an old proverb that says that the world will give us what we ask for. That is true in the feedback phase. In this phase, people start to treat us how we act. When we act like nobody cares about us and that we are the scum of the earth, people often oblige with harsh treatment and behavior. When we treat ourselves with respect and demand it from our peers, they often respond accordingly. In this phase, we realize that our performance has confirmed exactly what we initially believed about ourselves.

Once the confirmation is made, the final phase of the P3 Series is the "syndication." In this final phase, we become controlled by the cycle and often shape our self-esteem, self-image, personality, performance, and external appearance to fit that belief. There are plenty of strategies to fix and shape that self-image in order to live a more positive and prosperous version of yourself, but you're going to have to keep reading for those.

THE P3 SERIES
PURPOSE. POWER. PERFORMANCE

MAKEUP PHASE

WE SHAPE OUR SELF-ESTEEM AND HOW WE FEEL ABOUT OURSELVES

PERFORMANCE PHASE

WE PORTRAY WHATEVER SELF-IMAGE THAT WE CARRY

FEEDBACK PHASE

OUR PERFORMANCE CONFIRMS WHAT WE PREVIOUSLY BELIEVED ABOUT OURSELVES

SYNDICATION PHASE

WE BECOME CONTROLLED BY THE CYCLE AND SHAPE OUR ENTIRE BEING TO FIT THAT INITIAL BELIEF

INTERLUDE

WAYNE'S STORY

There's this one guy I know who can testify to how big of an effect self-talk can have on your life. One of my best friends, Dewayne (we call him "Wayne" for short) calls it the "Power of YET!" If you were to meet Wayne today, you wouldn't believe that he once contemplated suicide or that he ever considered giving up on his dreams. Wayne is a guy who has used this "power" to change his outlook on life and to adjust his "performance" to one that is positive and influential.

Wayne is the only child of a single mother, raised in the southwest corner of Georgia. He knows his father, but they didn't have the best relationship in Wayne's adolescence. Wayne spent a lot of time at his cousins' and friends' house due to his mom's busy work schedule. Despite being the baby of the family, Wayne developed rather quickly. By age eight, he was definitely a "husky" kid.

After an incident at a family cookout where an older cousin called attention to how much he had on his plate, Wayne became very self-conscious about his size. He often didn't eat in public and would wear baggy clothing to hide how big he truly was. As Wayne started to mature, he noticed that things were tight financially at his house. His mom was already working two jobs and still struggling to make ends meet. Wayne started to feel like a burden. Wayne started to have that ultimate negative thought. "Maybe things would be better if I wasn't here." With Wayne's self-esteem at an all-time low and his faith fading fast, his mother noticed the change.

She came to his bedroom one evening after not seeing Wayne mostly all day. He came down only to see his grandma, but not for dinner or family movie night. When she found him sitting on the floor, hugging his knees, she came in and sat beside him. Wayne and his mother had a good relationship and could talk about anything. They had a long conversation and she told him that no matter what happens, she will always love him and that he is not and never will be a burden. Then, she leaned in to give him a hug. She stood up to leave, but as she left, Wayne's mother dropped one of her favorite phrases, "Hey! We ain't made it YET, but we on the way!"

Despite his size, Wayne loved sports and was a very active kid. He played baseball, basketball, and football throughout his youth and into school sports. As a big kid he wasn't very athletic or talented, but he played hard. Wayne enjoyed the competitiveness of the games but after the talent gap widened too much in baseball, he gave that up. Wayne continued to play basketball and football and as he matured, so did his ability.

Wayne eventually became a decent high school player but received no offers to play college ball. To say he was disappointed would be an understatement. He lost his confidence and his self-belief that he was good enough to play. He wouldn't even participate in P.E. class on free days. After noticing that Wayne had received a 70 in P.E. on his midterm, his football coach called him to his office. It's never a good thing when Coach Hamilton calls you to his office, especially in the middle of the day.

Coach Hamilton was about 6'2, 230 lbs. and had a very raspy but boisterous voice. When he spoke, it got your attention. Especially when he has that scowl on his face and he goes, "HEY! WHAT ARE YOU DOING?!" Unfortunately for Wayne, that was exactly how their conversation started. As soon as Wayne turned the corner into Coach Hamilton's office, his booming voice hit Wayne like a ton of bricks. "Hey man! What are you doing?!" Wayne greeted Coach

Hamilton with a head nod and "Sup Coach?" Hamilton frowned and replied, "Don't what's up me! You need to know what's up with this C in PE." Wayne sits down as he says with a sigh, "I don't... Coach Smith be tripping."

Coach Hamilton slammed the door and pulled up a chair. Wayne could tell by the look on Hamilton's face, that he was in trouble. Hamilton sat down and leaned forward to make sure he had Wayne's attention. "You know what your problem is," started Hamilton, "You're sitting up here feeling sorry for yourself, and I'm tired of looking at it. You're mad because you don't have any offers, but you don't realize that it is still early in the process and you won't be a top prospect," Hamilton explained. As Coach Hamilton continued to be brutally honest about Wayne's recruiting prospects, Wayne's confidence was depleting even further.

The conversation was so rough on Wayne's confidence that he started to tune Hamilton out. Just as he was about to get up and leave, Hamilton said something that caught Wayne's attention. "Look Wayne, I know it looks bad right now," started Hamilton, "but you're good enough to play college ball. You're going to get an offer at some point. You just don't have one YET!" Hamilton suggested a workout regimen for athletes looking to maintain and sent Wayne back to class. Wayne thanked Coach Hamilton and left with a renewed confidence and sense of purpose. He WAS good enough. He WILL get an offer to play somewhere. He just hasn't gotten one YET!

Coach Hamilton was right, and Wayne eventually got an offer to play football at Mercer University, in Macon, Georgia. They were starting a football program and wanted Wayne to join it. Wayne was ecstatic and on National Signing Day, his dreams of playing college football came true. Wayne had no idea that his life was about to change in ways beyond what color football uniform he wore. As Wayne settled in at Mercer, things started well. His freshman year went according to plan in the classroom and on the football field, but that was just the beginning.

Sophomore year was a breeze and Wayne was trending in the right direction. However, as Wayne started his junior year at Mercer, things started to change. His position coach changed the previous off-season, which resulted in Wayne losing significant playing time. Despite how hard Wayne worked or how many plays he made, he couldn't seem to earn his starting position back. Wayne had also started coursework in his program of study, and it was tougher than he expected. As Wayne struggled to keep his spot on the football field, his grades were slipping too. On top of all of that, things back home were getting worse. Wayne's mother had lost her job and was struggling financially. Wayne loved his mother more than anything in this world, and he felt guilt in a way. Here he was at this fancy private institution while his mother is struggling to survive. Wayne seriously contemplated dropping out. As Christmas break approached, Wayne packed up nearly all of his belongings and secretly planned to never return.

On the third day of his Christmas break, Wayne went to the grocery store for his mom. As he was looking for his mom's favorite ice cream, he ran into an old friend, Leanne. Wayne hadn't really announced his arrival into town and was trying to keep a low profile, so he had mixed feelings when he bumped into her. He had known Leanne for years, and they graduated high school together. When he left for school, she even bought him a copy of his favorite movie. They had been good friends but had not really spoken since they both left for college.

After exchanging pleasantries, Leanne asked how Wayne was doing. Wayne took a step back, took a deep breath, and told the truth. After telling Leanne what was truly going on, she did what any solid friend would do. She gave Wayne a hug and encouraged him to not give up. After giving Wayne a motivating yet stern lecture, similar to those he used to get from his mother, Leanne reassured Wayne that he was going to be alright.

As she walked away, she told Wayne, "You're going to figure everything out. You just ain't figured out how YET! Don't worry though because you will." Wayne smiled and waved. He was happy that he had bumped into Leanne and needed that encouragement. He wasn't going to drop out after all. He was also going to find a way to help his mom. He was going to get his spot back, too, they just didn't know it YET!

Wayne was right! Heading into his senior year, Wayne trained harder than ever. He worked out two, and sometimes three, times a day. He was determined to earn his starting spot back.

Wayne not only won back his starting spot on the team - he even led the team in interceptions through the first five games of that season. Wayne also improved his status in the classroom. He found a tutor that he could relate to and started to get the help he needed.

Wayne's grades returned to the Dean's List stature that he had become accustomed to and he was primed to graduate with honors. He also found a way to help his mother financially. Once football season was over, Wayne signed up for work study to lower the tuition burden for him and his mother. He also found a part time job in the local city to make enough money to pay his car insurance, making that one less bill for his mom to worry about. Wayne's biggest help, however, came on his graduation day.

As he walked across the stage to receive his diploma, the president of Mercer University offered Wayne a paid graduate assistantship in the athletic department. Not only was he going to grad school for free, but he was getting paid to do it! Wayne was overcome with joy as he broke the news to his mom and they both hugged and cried happy tears. Wayne wiped his face and then patted his mother's, being sure not to mess up her makeup. Wayne handed his mother the diploma that he had just earned and told her what she had always told him, "Hey! we ain't made it YET, but we on the way!"

**DAILY DOSES
OF POSITIVITY**

PART IV

DAILY DOSES OF POSITIVITY

"Seek. And. Accept...

CRITICAL feedback!"

What Wayne realized is that his thoughts, beliefs, and actions aligned with negativity, so he got negative results. Once he became optimistic and started using the Power of YET, his life started to change. The Power of YET is not a magic trick. It is the result of daily practice and the intentional implementation of certain techniques and strategies to improve your self-talk.

I want to take this time to acknowledge that I am not a mental health professional, but these are strategies that have had proven success and are common practice for those striving to develop a growth mindset. Wayne's story is an example of how those daily doses of positivity can alter your perspective.

According to a 2017 study conducted by the National Science Foundation, we have nearly 24,000 negative thoughts a day. With that sort of negativity floating around all day, there is clearly more to having a growth mindset than saying you have one. It takes time and a consistent plan. There are four tactics that could help us develop a growth mindset and fight off the negativity. We must develop learning strategies, seek and accept critical feedback, have better emotional intelligence, and make better decisions.

First and foremost, we must believe in ourselves. We must believe in our ability to figure it out. Think about it... we've survived 100% of our bad days so far. No matter how rough our circumstances may have looked, we found a way through. It wasn't easy in any sense of the word, but we made it. So, when times get rough again or when we get frustrated, we must find a way to curb that negative energy. We need to develop the mental fortitude that allows us to focus on solutions and strategies and not the problems and issues.

Secondly, we must be able to seek and accept critical feedback. Seek. And. Accept... CRITICAL feedback! That is a tough challenge for almost anyone. Even those with the most ambitious growth mindset struggle to seek and accept that sort of helpful feedback. However, if we truly want to grow and become the best version of ourselves then we need constructive criticism. Sometimes we need an outside perspective on what we're doing and how we're doing it.

Plus, we all need a mentor. According to Dave Ramsey, "A good mentor will be empathetic and kind because they've been down the same road you're on. They know what it's like to fail, get back up, and keep going." A mentor is someone who can provide the necessary feedback to push us out of our comfort zones. Once we are out of our comfort zone, we start to grow. The biggest obstacle for most people is accepting this feedback with the right attitude and knowing which parts of it to apply. That skill comes over time, but the first step is to be willing to seek and accept that sort of critical feedback.

This is not a sermon but an empathetic appeal to you to reconsider your current mindset to encourage and assist you in propelling forward into your best self. This is not a "pull yourself up by your bootstraps" type of message. We must know how far and how much to push our abilities in the right situation. We must be able to handle the distance that is naturally created between who we currently are and the people who knew the old us. We also need to be aware of how our environment affects us spiritually, physically, and emotionally and find ways to make sure that we take care of our mental health in a way that can sustain the challenge of successfully operating with a growth mindset.

We must hold ourselves accountable every day. When trying to develop our growth mindset, we must make better decisions on a daily basis. Every day, we make decisions that will affect our future in a big way. I'm not saying that we should be so cautious as to become stagnant, but I'm suggesting that we be more strategic in the moves we make. We need to be cautious when things don't seem aligned with our goals and values or when we can't handle the obligations. If we were with the homies, we would warn each other to "never get tricked out your position." The same is true in our personal and professional lives, as well as with our mental health. We must be efficient and be sure to maximize opportunities when they present themselves. I once heard a motivational speaker say that you "must take advantage of an opportunity of a lifetime during the lifetime of the opportunity." We must be strategic but can't be afraid to make a move. We must trust ourselves and the plan we all individually received from God.

FINAL THOUGHT

PART V

FINAL THOUGHT

When Wayne was struggling through college, he searched high and low for guidance in his situation. During that time, he ran across this book called *Think and Grow Rich* by Napoleon Hill. The book is all about growth mindset and self-regulation. It describes how we all have the mental capacity to create whatever destiny we choose. We must make the necessary moves and sacrifices to achieve the success we want to acquire. In this book, there's a positive affirmation that Wayne sparked Wayne's belief and positivity.

This affirmation is what led Wayne toward discovering the Power of YET. This affirmation is so powerful that Wayne still uses it daily. Ever since Wayne first shared this quote with me, I have loved it and have incorporated these positive words into my daily routine. This affirmation exudes the Power of YET and I want to share it with you too.

DAY BY DAY

IN EVERY WAY

I'M GETTING BETTER AND BETTER!

Go back... Don't just read that statement. Say it! Not in your head.

Out loud! Say it with pride! Say it like you mean it! Say it like you hope to improve in every capacity of your life every single day. Even if it's just one percent. One percent better each day is better than zero percent better for 100 days straight. Get up and go to your mirror. Look at yourself and remind yourself how great you are. Say this affirmation with passion! Say it like you mean it!

<u>DAY BY DAY</u>

IN EVERY WAY

I'M GETTING BETTER AND BETTER!

DAY BY DAY

<u>IN EVERY WAY</u>

I'M GETTING BETTER AND BETTER!

DAY BY DAY

IN EVERY WAY

<u>I'M GETTING BETTER AND BETTER!</u>

Ahh... Don't you feel so empowered? Don't you feel like you can conquer anything put in your way? Don't you feel proud of the things that you have accomplished? Don't you feel a sense of pride about the things you experienced that once seemed negative, but now serve as wealthy experience on your journey? If not, keep saying that affirmation. Keep reminding yourself that this is a long journey. Keep reminding yourself that you will accomplish everything you desire and have the impact you envision; you just haven't figured it out YET! That's okay though because day by day in every way, you're getting better and better!

Just in case somebody hasn't told you in a while, I want to remind you that you can be whoever you want to be if you work for it. You can be a doctor, lawyer, social media influencer, athlete, teacher, or global celebrity as long as you combine **belief** with **work**.

I know you're going to work hard physically to achieve those goals. My challenge, however, is to work on developing your growth mindset. Use the strategies shared in this book to help you grow in the areas where your confidence seems to fade. Share this information with your loved ones and affirm their dreams and goals as well. When you share what you know and you help restore mental strength and positivity into your social circle, it helps everyone involved. It helps them in obvious ways, and that good deed will return to you. You should enjoy pouring into the people around you, but that is not my point here. By holding your peers and associates accountable, you improve your chances of acquiring a strong growth mindset for yourself. Iron sharpens iron, and when positivity flows through multiple channels of your life, you feel better.

If you trust the plan and vision that God has for you, commit to the process of refining your mindset, and work to change your self-talk then you will live a more positive and purpose-filled life. I challenge you to be willing to accept the challenge of striving to be the best version of yourself on a daily. I know things won't always be easy, but I know that you will make it through. On your bad days, when things seem the absolute worst, I challenge you to be courageous enough to keep fighting. Mary Anne Radmacher once said, "Courage doesn't always roar. Sometimes courage is that quiet voice at the end of the day saying that I will try again tomorrow." So be courageous and know that you're getting better every day, but it's going to take some time and some intentional work. You are smart, you are strong, you are capable of figuring things out. You have remarkable gifts to share with the world, and we are all waiting on you. We are excited to see what you do and accomplish, even if you don't know what that is... **YET!**

Good luck and Godspeed.

CPSIA information can be obtained
at www.ICGtesting.com
Printed in the USA
JSHW051854230522
26049JS00007BA/221

9 780578 293059